PRACTICE Q R BLUE PROFESSIONAL DEVELOPER CERTIFICATION CASED BASED – LATEST EDITION

BLUE PRISM PROFESSIONAL DEVELOPER CERTIFICATION CASE BASED PRACTICE QUESTIONS - LATEST EDITION 2023

First edition. April 5, 2023.

ISBN: 979-8215017272

Written by Exam OG.

EXAM OG

Certificate Introduction:

We are pleased to present the latest edition of "Practice Questions for Blue Prism Professional Developer Certification Case-Based." This book is designed to help aspiring Blue Prism developers prepare for the certification exam by providing a comprehensive collection of practice questions and case-based scenarios.

As the demand for skilled Blue Prism developers continues to grow, earning the Professional Developer Certification has become a vital credential for professionals in this field. This certification validates the candidate's proficiency in designing, developing, and deploying Blue Prism solutions.

To help candidates achieve success in the certification exam, this book includes a variety of case-based scenarios and practice questions that cover all aspects of the exam syllabus. The questions are designed to test the candidate's understanding of key concepts, as well as their ability to apply them in real-world situations.

This latest edition has been updated with the latest exam patterns and includes additional practice questions that will help candidates gain a deeper understanding of the concepts covered in the exam. Our goal is to provide candidates with the most up-to-date and comprehensive study material, which will help them pass the certification exam with ease.

We believe that this book will be an invaluable resource for aspiring Blue Prism developers looking to improve their chances of success in the certification exam. We wish you all the best in your certification journey!

PRACTICE QUESTIONS

Question 1:

The ABC Bank has implemented a Blue Prism automation process to handle customer requests for loan approvals. The automation involves logging into the bank's loan approval system, checking the customer's credit score, and approving or rejecting the loan based on the score. During the automation, Blue Prism encountered an error and was unable to identify an element in the loan approval system.

What sort of exception is generated when Blue Prism encounters an unmatched element in the ABC Bank's loan approval system?

A) Business Exceptions

B) Exceptions to the Rules in the Computer System

C) Internal Exceptions

D) Invalid element exception

Explanation:

Answer - C

Whenever Blue Prism is unable to determine the identity of an element, it generates an internal exception, as stated in the MCQ. Therefore, the correct answer is C. Option A, Business Exceptions, are thrown when input data is missing or erroneous, which is not the case in this scenario. Option B, Exceptions to the Rules in the Computer System, are thrown as a result of the target system's inactivity, which is not the cause of the error in this scenario. Option D, Invalid element exception, is not supported by Blue Prism, as mentioned in the MCQ. Hence, the correct answer is C, Internal Exceptions.

Question 2:

A banking institution has implemented a Blue Prism automation process to handle loan application submissions. The automation involves the submission of the application, checking for completeness and accuracy, and then marking the application as "Deferred" in the work queue if further information is needed from the customer.

What is true regarding a loan application case that has been marked as "Deferred" in the work queue in the Blue Prism automation process?

A) On the new date, this case has been chosen for processing.

B) The instance has been chosen for deletion by hand.

C) The case will be forever deleted from the system once it has been resolved in Blue Prism.

D) The case was resolved favorably.

Explanation:

Answer - A

When an item in a work queue is marked as "Deferred," it means that processing of the item has been postponed until a later date. Therefore, option A is the correct answer. Option B, manual deletion, is incorrect as there is no indication in the scenario that the case has been selected for manual deletion. Option C, removal from the system permanently, is incorrect as the deferred case will still be available for processing at a later date. Option D, resolved favorably, is also incorrect as the case has been deferred due to incomplete or inaccurate information, indicating that it has not been resolved favorably yet.

Question 3:

A company has implemented a Blue Prism automation process to handle customer requests for product information. The automation involves logging into the company's information system, searching for the requested product information, and adding tags to the work queue for further processing.

In Blue Prism automation, which of the following claims about tags and task queue filtering is accurate?

A) Use an asterisk (*) to discover "any other characters," while a question mark (?) finds "any single character" in a tag.

B) Asterisk and question mark characters are used to look for "any single character" and "any other character," respectively, in a tag.

C) The next item move in Blue Prism work queues does not allow tags for filtering.

D) None of the above.

Explanation:

Answer - A

As stated in the MCQ, in Blue Prism automation, the asterisk (*) is used to find "any other characters," while the question mark (?) is used to find "any single character" in a tag. Therefore, option A is the correct answer. Option B is incorrect because it states the opposite, with the asterisk being used to search for "any single character" and the question mark being used for "any other characters." Option C is also incorrect because Blue Prism work queues do support tags to be used for filtering. Option D, none of the above, is incorrect because option A is the correct answer.

Question 4:

A company has implemented a Blue Prism automation process to handle customer orders for a product. The automation involves logging into the company's order management system, checking the order status, and updating the status in the work queue for tracking purposes.

Which of the following is accurate regarding the work queue in the Blue Prism automation process for customer orders?

A) The state of a work case may be updated multiple times.

B) A work queue object's status can only be altered at the time the item is added.

C) Deleted work queue status.

D) Not any of the above.

Explanation:

Answer - A

As stated in the MCQ, in Blue Prism automation, the status of a work queue item can be updated multiple times. Therefore, option A is the correct answer. Option B is incorrect as it suggests that the status of an item can only be changed at the moment it is added, which is not true in Blue Prism. Option C, deleted work queue status, is not a valid option as once a status has been added to a work queue, it cannot be removed; only updates can be made. Option D, not any of the above, is incorrect as option A is the correct answer.

Question 5:

A company has implemented a Blue Prism automation process to handle customer complaints. The automation involves logging into the company's complaint management system, adding the complaint to the work queue, and assigning a priority to the complaint.

After a customer complaint has been added to the work queue in the Blue Prism automation process, which method of the work queue object can be used to change its priority?

A) Establish Priorities

B) Most Urgent Priority Update

C) Rearrange priorities

D) None

Explanation:

Answer - A

In Blue Prism automation, the priority of a work queue item can be updated or altered using the "Set Priority" action in the "Establish Priorities" method. Therefore, option A is the correct answer. Option B, "Most Urgent Priority Update," is not a valid method in Blue Prism. Option C, "Rearrange Priorities," is also not a valid method in Blue Prism for changing the priority of a work queue item. Option D, "None," is incorrect as there is a method available to change the priority of a work queue item.

Question 6:

A company has implemented a Blue Prism automation process to handle customer orders for a product. The automation involves logging into the company's order management system, checking the order status, and updating the order status in the work queue for tracking purposes.

How can the encryption method used by Blue Prism's task queue be changed or disabled so that the task queue can be decrypted?

A) Operation Room

B) System Manager

C) Process Studio

D) Object Studio

Explanation:

Answer - B

The System Manager module can be used to alter the encryption algorithm in the work queue or turn it off entirely to decrypt the task queue. Therefore, option B is the correct answer. Option A, Operation Room, is incorrect as it is not a valid module in Blue Prism. Option C, Process Studio, is incorrect as it is used to create business logic and rules. Option D, Object Studio, is incorrect as it is used to "spy" on the target app's elements and build actions to interact with those elements.

Question 7:

A company has implemented a Blue Prism automation process to handle customer requests for a product. The automation involves multiple steps in the process, and the developer only has access to a single Blue Prism license.

Which type of work queue configuration in Blue Prism automation would be most suitable if there are many stages in the automation process and at least one week should pass between each step?

A) Dividing the job into two parts and running it on two different robots and computers.

B) Putting all of a case's relevant information into a single Work Queue and waiting one week for it to be handled.

C) Distributing the task between people and the Blue Prism robot.

D) Blue Prism does not support multi-step processes being automated.

Explanation:

Answer - B

When there are numerous steps in the automation process, and at least one week should elapse between each step, the most appropriate form of work queue configuration is to put everything related to a case into a single Work Queue and wait a week to handle it. Therefore, option B is the correct answer. Option A, splitting the process task across two robots and executing it on separate computers, is not a viable option as it would require the purchase of additional licenses. Option C, splitting the workload between the Blue Prism robot and humans, is also not a viable option as it would require human interaction to automate the entire process. Option D, it is not possible to automate multi-step procedures with Blue Prism, is incorrect as Blue Prism has the ability to streamline operations with multiple moving parts using the Multi-Part Processes - Deferring and Multiple Queues technique of work queue management.

Question 8:

A company has implemented a Blue Prism automation process to handle customer orders for a product. The automation involves logging into the company's order management system, checking the order status, and updating the order status in the work queue for tracking purposes.

Which of the following choices is not a part of Blue Prism's task queue design methodology?

A) Multiple queues and delays in multi-step procedures.

B) Relationships between parents and children in waiting areas.

C) Queue-filling Workflow Systems.

D) The input of work case items by hand.

Explanation:

Answer - D

Among the options given, the one that does not belong to the work queue design methodology in Blue Prism is the input of work case items by hand. Therefore, option D is the correct answer. Option A, delaying and multiple queues in multi-step processes, is a part of the Multi-Part Processes - Deferring and Multiple Queues technique of work queue management. Option B, relationships between parents and children in waiting areas, is used in situations where two or more work queue items must be associated with a single request. Option C, queue-filling Workflow Systems, is a part of the work queue design methodology in Blue Prism as it is used to fill work queues.

Question 9:

A company has implemented a Blue Prism automation process to handle customer orders for a product. The automation involves logging into the company's order management system, checking the order status, and updating the order status in the work queue for tracking purposes.

Which of the following choices is not a part of Blue Prism's task queue design methodology?

A) Multiple queues and delays in multi-step procedures.

B) Relationships between parents and children in waiting areas.

C) Queue-filling Workflow Systems.

D) The input of work case items by hand.

Explanation:

Answer - D

The one that does not belong to the work queue design methodology in Blue Prism is the input of work case items by hand. Therefore, option D is the correct answer. Option A, delaying and multiple queues in multi-step processes, is a part of the Multi-Part Processes - Deferring and Multiple Queues technique of work queue management. Option B, relationships between parents and children in waiting areas, is used in situations where two or more work queue items must be associated with a single request. Option C, queue-filling Workflow Systems, is a part of the work queue design methodology in Blue Prism as it is used to fill work queues.

Question 10:

In the Blue Prism automation process implemented by a company, the navigation flow involves launching the application and then attaching to a subpage. The question pertains to the correctness of the execution of this navigation flow and asks which of the options provided is true regarding it.

A) The page was carried out without a hitch.

B) Attach must be set up before launch.

C) A failure to attach the navigation stage occurs.

D) An error occurs during the launch of the navigator stage.

Explanation:

Answer - C

Regarding the execution of the subpage navigation flow in the Blue Prism automation process, a failure to attach the navigation stage occurs. Therefore, option C is the correct answer. Option A, the page was carried out without a hitch, is not correct as the question mentions that there is a navigation flow involving two stages, and an exception could occur in either of the stages. Option B, attach must be set up before launch, is also not correct as there is no set sequence in which attach and launch must be configured. Option D, an error occurs during the launch of the navigator stage, is also not correct as the launch does not generate an exception when navigating to a new stage.

Question 11:

A Blue Prism automation process encounters an error on a given page, and steps need to be taken to locate the source of the error.

Which of the following steps is NOT used to identify the error's cause on the specified page?

A) Taking necessary measures.

B) Making repairs.

C) Getting back to work.

D) Throwing exceptions.

Explanation:

Answer - D

The question is asking which of the options provided is NOT a step used to locate the source of an error on a given page. Option A, taking necessary measures, is a step used to locate the source of an error. Option B, making repairs, is also a step used to locate and fix the source of an error. Option C, getting back to work, is a step taken after the error has been located and resolved. Therefore, the correct answer is D, throwing exceptions, as throwing exceptions is not a step used to locate the source of an error. Exceptions are raised when an error occurs, and they can be handled using exception handling techniques such as the Exception Block.

Question 12:

Blue Prism's exception handling is a critical aspect of its automation process. During the execution of a process, an error is encountered when the system is unable to locate a specified element. What type of exception will be thrown by Blue Prism?

A) Business Exceptions

B) Exceptions to the Rules in the Computer System

C) Internal Exceptions

D) Invalid element exception

Explanation:

Answer - C

Option A is incorrect because Business Exceptions are thrown when input data is missing or erroneous. Option B is also incorrect because system exceptions are thrown when the target system is inactive. Option D is not a valid exception type supported by Blue Prism. The correct answer is C, as Blue Prism generates an internal exception when it is unable to determine the identity of an element.

Question 13:

A company has implemented a Blue Prism automation process to perform a complex task that involves multiple subpages. In the event that an exception is thrown during the execution of one of the subpages, where in the process design should the logic for retrying be implemented?

A) Business Objects

B) Subpages

C) Home Page

D) Nowhere

Explanation:

Answer - A

By implementing the retry exception logic in separate pages, Business Objects can take precautions against infinite loops and unnecessary retries. Option B is not correct as the decision regarding retry logic needs to be made at the process design phase, not the subpage level. Choice C is incorrect because retry logic cannot be handled at the Home Page level. Option D is also incorrect as retry mechanism can and should be implemented in the process design to handle exceptions.

Question 14:

A company is implementing a Blue Prism automation process to navigate a subpage of an application. During the process, an exception occurs when attempting to attach or launch the application, resulting in the following error: "Target application not found (Internal: failed to perform step 1 in navigation stage 'Attach' on page 'attach (or launch)')."

Which of the following is the most likely cause of the error?

A) The Navigate stage was not utilized in the application's attachment process.

B) More than one element with the same footprint was discovered in the target application.

C) The target application was not started.

D) It's an internal error in the Blue Prism product.

Explanation:

Answer - C

This is because the error message states that the target application was not found, and the most common reason for this is that the application was not started. Option A is incorrect because using the Navigate stage is required to attach to the target application. Option B is also incorrect because this error message is specific to the target application not being found, not to there being multiple elements with the same footprint. Option D is also incorrect because the error message specifically states that it is an Internal error in the navigation stage of the process, not an internal Blue Prism error.

Question 15:

A Blue Prism automation process was running smoothly until it suddenly stopped and displayed an empty exception dialogue box. The team is unsure about what went wrong and how to troubleshoot it.

Which of the following options could explain the issue?

A) The properties of the unhandled Exception stage were left blank.

B) It was caused by a bug in Blue Prism's internal code.

C) The process terminated with an internal exception.

D) The preserve check was not used properly.

Explanation:

Answer - A

Option A is the correct choice. When the properties of an unhandled Exception stage are left empty, a generic exception is thrown. This can cause issues for subsequent exception handling and can make it difficult to troubleshoot the problem.

Option B is incorrect because it is unlikely that the issue is caused by a bug in Blue Prism's internal code.

Option C is not a definitive explanation for the issue and does not provide any insight into the cause of the problem.

Option D is also incorrect as the preserve check is not related to the exception dialogue box being empty.

Question 16:

A company has a large project that requires the involvement of multiple developers. Which of the following approaches is the most appropriate?

A) Dividing the process into its component parts according to their intended uses

B) Creating multiple shifts for developers to access the process and objects

C) Using a unified login for all developers

D) Designing the project to allow multiple developers to work on the same project simultaneously, while working with various objects within the object layer.

Explanation:

Answer - D

Designing the project to allow multiple developers to work on the same project simultaneously is the most efficient and effective approach. This allows for scalability and the ability to handle multiple tasks at the same time while ensuring that all objects within the object layer are accessible to all developers.

Option A is not the best option because dividing the process can lead to integration issues.

Option B is not the best choice because it is not an efficient use of resources.

Choice C is not a recommended practice because Blue Prism discourages the practice of exchanging user IDs.

Therefore, the correct answer is option D.

Question 17:

A software development team is implementing a new automation project using the Blue Prism platform. During which stage of the development process should the team create a build review checklist for the robot?

A) Planning and Design

B) Development and Coding

C) Testing and Quality Assurance

D) Deployment and Launch

Explanation:

Answer - B

As part of the development and coding stage of the Blue Prism deployment approach, the software development team should create a build review checklist to ensure that the robot is developed according to best practices and meets the project requirements. This checklist should be established during unit testing to catch any errors or issues before the robot is launched into production. Therefore, option B is the best choice.

Question 18:

In Blue Prism, how many labels or tags can be associated with a case in a work queue?

A) 1

B) 2

C) 0

D) There is no limit

Explanation:

Answer - D

In Blue Prism, tags are used to classify and filter objects, including cases in work queues. Tags are separated by semicolons and there is no upper limit to the number of tags that can be added to a case. Therefore, the correct answer is D, as there is no restriction on the number of tags that can be associated with a case in a work queue.

Question 19:

In which Blue Prism module do we configure web service actions in order to allow for automatic failover if one server goes down?

A) Control Room

B) Object Studio

C) Process Studio

D) System Manager

Explanation:

Answer - A

Blue Prism's Control Room offers a variety of administration tools, including the ability to manage system configurations and schedules, and the ability to define and monitor control room access. Additionally, automatic failover functionality for web service actions may be configured in the control room.

Hence, Option A is the correct choice.

Choice B, Object Studio is not correct since it's used to design, build, and maintain business objects.

Choice C, Process Studio is also not correct since it's used to design the process flow for automation.

Choice D, System Manager is not correct since it's used to perform system management tasks such as configuring resources and license allocation.

Question 20:

A company has developed a process in Blue Prism that they want to expose as a web service for external use. What is the most important requirement for this process to be exposed as a web service?

A) The name of the published process should only contain alphabetic and numeric characters.

B) The process should have a code stage in it for web service configuration.

C) The process should be configured for web service in the Control Room.

D) Exposing Blue Prism components as web services is not recommended.

Explanation:

Answer - A

The correct answer is A because the name of the published process must only contain alphanumeric letters (i.e., no punctuation or space characters) in order to be exposed as a web service.

Choice B is incorrect because the code stage is typically helpful when dealing with a COM object in a Microsoft Windows environment, and it is not required for making a Blue Prism module accessible via a web service.

Choice C is also incorrect because no setup is needed to make the process or object accessible as a web service.

Choice D is incorrect because Blue Prism modules can be exposed as web services, but the name of the process must comply with specific naming standards.

Question 21:

A manufacturing company wants to integrate a new third-party inventory management system into their existing Blue Prism system. They want to make the inventory data easily accessible for their employees through the Blue Prism interface.

In what way can the new inventory system be made accessible in Blue Prism's Process Studio?

A) Processes

B) Business Objects categories

C) Steps,

D) Texts

Explanation:

Answer - B

The correct choice is B because when a new third-party service is added to the Blue Prism system manager, it becomes available as a business object in Process Studio. The employees can then access the inventory data through the actions within the business object.

Choice A is incorrect because Processes describe a sequence of activities in a business, but do not necessarily provide access to third-party systems.

Choice C is incorrect because steps are actions within a business object or process, not a means of accessing a new third-party system.

Choice D is incorrect because texts are not used to access third-party systems in Blue Prism.

Question 22:

What does WSDL stand for in the context of Blue Prism?

A) Web Service Description Language

B) Web Service Definition Language

C) Web Service Design Language

D) Web Service Development Language

Explanation:

Answer - A

WSDL stands for "Web Service Description Language" in the context of Blue Prism. It is an XML format that describes the functionality provided by a web service and the method of communication with it. It provides a common way for developers to describe and discover web services, which facilitates interoperability between different software systems. Option B, C, and D are not the correct answers, as they do not accurately reflect the purpose and function of WSDL in Blue Prism.

Question 23:

A company is integrating a third-party web service into their Blue Prism automation solution. They need to configure the authentication method to access the web service. Which of the following authentication methods is not supported by Blue Prism?

A) Authentication using Internet Protocol

B) Certificate-based authentication

C) Username and password as part of the HTTP header

D) WS-Security authentication

Explanation:

Answer - D

Blue Prism supports authentication using IP, certificate-based authentication, and username/password as part of the HTTP header. However, it does not support WS-Security authentication.

Question 24:

In an organization, Blue Prism is being used to automate various processes. A team is working on integrating these processes as web services and exposing them to the external world. There are a total of 5 different processes that have been exposed over the internet. How many Blue Prism licenses are required to connect to all five exposed processes at once?

A) 5

B) 8

C) 3

D) 1

Explanation:

Answer - C

Option A is incorrect because exposing processes as web services does not consume Blue Prism licenses.

Option B is incorrect because it is not possible to run five processes simultaneously with a Blue Prism license count of 8.

Each request to an exposed process will require a new session, which will consume one Blue Prism license per session. As a result, the number of licenses required to connect to all five exposed processes at once would be 3 (one for each process).

Option D is incorrect because the number of processes being run should be proportional to the number of Blue Prism licenses in use.

Question 25:

An organization is using Blue Prism for automating their business processes. They have implemented three background business objects to be exposed as web services. How many sessions will be auto-initialized in a resource PC when these three business objects are connected simultaneously?

A) 0

B) 1

C) 3

D) The same number of calls

Explanation:

Answer - C

Since the three background business objects are made available as web services, they require licenses to operate, and hence option A is incorrect.

Using one license to operate three auto-initialized objects is not possible, making option B incorrect.

For consuming a single object from a web service, only one session is required per resource PC. However, since three objects in background run mode are made available as web services, three sessions will be auto-initialized on the same resource PC so that they can communicate with each other simultaneously, making option C the correct answer.

Option D is incorrect as the number of sessions auto-initialized and the license used are directly proportional to each other.

Question 26:

A company is integrating three "Exclusive" business objects as web services into their Blue Prism system. If they want to auto-initialize and connect to all three objects simultaneously, how many licenses will be required?

A) None

B) One

C) Three

D) The same amount of licenses as the number of calls

Explanation:

Answer - C

Using a business object requires a license, so option A is incorrect.

Connecting three business objects simultaneously would require three licenses, so option B is incorrect.

Therefore, the correct answer is C - three licenses are needed to auto-initialize and connect to all three business objects as web services at the same time.

Option D is incorrect because the number of licenses needed is not related to the number of calls made to the web services.

Question 27:

A company wants to integrate a Blue Prism business object as a web service to allow external applications to access it. However, they are unsure how many different ways there are to initiate a connection to the web service implementation of the business object. Which of the following options correctly describes the available options for initiating a connection?

A) 0

B) 1

C) 2

D) Many

Explanation:

Answer - C

Blue Prism business objects can be exposed as web services using two different initialization methods. The calling application is responsible for managing the session generation process in its own code. This allows for multiple requests to be processed in parallel within the same session. Therefore, the correct answer is C. Option A is incorrect since there are at least two different ways to initiate a connection. Option B is incorrect since there are two different ways to initiate a connection. Option D is incorrect since the number of ways to initiate a connection is limited to two.

Question 28:

A company is implementing Blue Prism for its business processes. The IT team is discussing the run modes that are available in Blue Prism. They want to choose a run mode that allows several sessions to share a machine's resources. Which run mode should they choose?

A) foreground

B) exclusive

C) background

D) background and none at all.

Explanation:

Answer - C

In Blue Prism, several types of background sessions can be created on a computer using the background run mode. A single computer cannot simultaneously support two separate foreground sessions. It is also not possible to have a background session concurrent with a front session, and a single computer cannot host two mutually exclusive sessions at the same time. Therefore, the correct answer is C, the background run mode.

Question 29:

A software developer needs to generate auto-generated code for a third-party online service. Which of the following tools should they NOT use for this purpose?

A) wsdl.exe

B) SOAP.exe

C) SOAPUI.exe

D) Vs.exe

Explanation:

Answer - B

Wsdl.exe and WSewsdl3.exe are tools that can be used to generate auto-generated code for third-party online services. Therefore, option A is not the answer. The SOAPUI.exe tool is used to test SOAP and REST web services, so it is not appropriate for generating auto-generated code. Therefore, option C is not the answer. Vs.exe is a shortened version of Visual Studio, and it often comes pre-loaded with wsdl.exe and WSewsdl3.exe, so it can be used for generating auto-generated code. Therefore, option D is not the answer. The correct answer is option B, as it is not a tool that can be used for generating auto-generated code for third-party online services.

Question 30:

A client is integrating Blue Prism's web services for their business. Which authentication mechanism should they use to secure their web services?

A) An Overview of HTTP Authentication

B) WS-Security system.

C) Authentication with certificates

D) Ip Based authentication

Explanation:

Answer - A

Blue Prism's web services are secured through HTTP authentication, which is why choice A is correct. WS-Security authentication, certificate-based authentication, and IP-based authentication are not supported by Blue Prism, so options B, C, and D are incorrect.

Question 31:

A company uses Blue Prism to automate its processes. They need to link to the second tab in Google Chrome. Choose the appropriate navigation stage setting to achieve this.

A) Chrome.exe, with a child index of 0

B) Chrome.exe, with a child index of 1

C) Chrome.exe, with a child index of 2

D) Chrome.exe, with a child index of 3

Explanation:

Answer - C

Answer choice A and B are incorrect since they refer to the parent process of Google Chrome and not the tab.

Choice C is correct because the child index of 2 refers to the second tab in Google Chrome.

Choice D is incorrect since Google Chrome is not identified using the ".exe" extension and there are no child indexes greater than 2 for the tabs.

Question 32:

In a web application, a user needs to extract data from a table and use it for further processing. Which of the following native actions of the Read stage in Blue Prism should be used to retrieve the values of the HTML table?

A) Get Table

B) Get Current Value

C) Get Description

D) Get Name

Explanation:

Answer - A

Option A is the correct answer since the Get Table native action of the Read stage in Blue Prism is used to retrieve a collection of all the HTML elements present in a table. This collection is then processed to obtain the required data.

Option B is incorrect since the Get Current Value native action of the Read stage is used to obtain the current value of a UI element, such as a text box, combo box, list view, current row, checkbox, etc.

Option C is incorrect since the Get Description native action of the Read stage is used to obtain the description of an Accessibility element.

Option D is incorrect since the Get Name native action of the Read stage is used to obtain the name of an Accessibility element.

Question 33:

In a web automation process, a button must be clicked to initiate a download. However, the download may take some time, and it is important to verify that it is complete before proceeding with the next step. Which of the following wait stages should be used in this scenario?

A) Wait for Document Ready

B) Wait for Page Idle

C) Wait for Text Exists

D) Wait for Image Exists

Explanation:

Answer - B

Option B is the correct answer because Wait for Page Idle ensures that no more network requests are active and the page has stopped loading. This is the appropriate wait stage for the download process to complete before proceeding to the next step.

Wait for Document Ready (A) checks whether the DOM is ready to interact with, and Wait for Text Exists (C) and Wait for Image Exists (D) are used to wait for the existence of specific text or image on a web page, and do not provide an appropriate wait stage for a download to complete.

Therefore, the answer is B.

Question 34:

A company is using Blue Prism's Application Modeller to automate their web application. They have identified an HTML element that they want to interact with. Which of the following is not an HTML attribute of the element that can be used in the Application Modeller tag?

A) Parent URL

B) Path

C) Style

D) Class Name

Explanation:

Answer - C

The other attributes listed, Parent URL, Path, and Class Name, are all HTML attributes that can be used in the Application Modeller tag. However, Style is not an HTML attribute, but rather a Win32 attribute. Therefore, it is not applicable to the HTML elements identified through the Application Modeller.

Question 35:

John, a Blue Prism developer, needs to dynamically update the information displayed on a web application using JavaScript. Which action in the navigate stage should he use to invoke the JavaScript function?

A) Insert JavaScript Fragment

B) Invoke

C) Call

D) Execute

Explanation:

Answer - B

Option A, Insert JavaScript Fragment, is not the correct action to use because it is used to incorporate minor JavaScript functions into an existing web application.

Option B, Invoke, is the correct answer because it allows you to call a JavaScript function defined in the HTML of the web page you are interacting with. This action can save time and simplify the process of updating the information displayed on a web application using JavaScript.

Options C and D, Call and Execute, are not supported by Blue Prism, so they are incorrect.

<u>**Question 36:**</u>

A company is looking to automate their mainframe application. Which of the following is the essential field required to initiate or attach to a mainframe application using Blue Prism?

A) Session Identifier

B) Mainframe Vendor

C) Server Name

D) Title

Explanation:

Answer - A

When initiating or attaching to a mainframe connection, the session identification must be provided, hence choice A is the best option. Blue Prism does not require a mainframe vendor for deployment or maintenance, so option B is not applicable. Option C is not accurate because Blue Prism does not require the server for startup or attachment. Choice D is wrong because the title is never used in the introduction or conclusion of Blue Prism.

<u>**Question 37:**</u>

A user is attempting to enter data into a text field on a web page using Blue Prism's automation capabilities. The user receives an error message indicating that the text entered is invalid. What action should the user take first to resolve the issue?

A) Verify that the text field exists on the web page.

B) Check that the correct value is being entered in the text field.

C) Ensure that the correct data type is being used to enter the text.

D) Validate that the correct HTML tag is being used to identify the text field.

Explanation:

Answer - B

The error message indicates that the entered text is invalid, the user should first verify that the correct value is being entered into the text field. It is feasible that the user is entering an incorrect value or format, or that the text field has a particular data requirement, such as a specific format or length.

Choice A is incorrect because if the text field did not exist, the user would receive a different error message.

Option C is incorrect because the error message does not imply that the user is employing the incorrect data type.

Choice D is incorrect because the user has already identified the text field; the issue is with the data being entered, not with the HTML tag identifying the text field.

Question 38:

In a company's finance department, a new Java-based application has been introduced that needs to be automated using Blue Prism. Which application management mode should be used to best integrate with this 64-bit Java application?

A) 64-bit internally

B) 32-bit externally

C) 64-bit externally

D) None of the above

Explanation:

Answer - C

Option A is incorrect because Blue Prism does not support 64-bit applications.

Option B is incorrect because the Program Manager interfaces with the target application in a background process. External, 32-bit mode is not used for the Application Manager process.

Option C is the correct answer because the Application Manager communicates with the target application while operating in a separate process. When running in 64-bit mode, the Application Manager process is always 32 bits.

Option D is incorrect because the answer is not related to the address size of the operating system or any extraneous factor.

Therefore, option C is the best choice for integrating Blue Prism with the new 64-bit Java application in the finance department.

Question 39:

You're automating a Java-based customer service application for a telecommunications company. You notice that some of the application's fields are hidden behind a dropdown menu, and you want to make sure that Blue Prism's Application Modeller Wizard doesn't pick up on this hidden code. What option should you select?

A) Descendtree

B) Ignoring and not showing

C) AncestryRelativesCount

D) Not Presenting

Explanation:

Answer - B

Choice A, Descendtree, is incorrect because this option would instruct Blue Prism to look through the full Program Model Tree for components in the target Java application, including hidden code.

Choice B, Ignoring and not showing, is the correct answer. This option tells Blue Prism's Application Modeller Wizard to ignore and not show any items in the Application Model Tree that have been flagged as "not showing."

Choice C, AncestryRelativesCount, is not relevant to this scenario and is therefore incorrect.

Choice D, Not Presenting, is also not a valid option in Blue Prism.

Therefore, the correct answer is B, Ignoring and not showing.

Question 40:

A company is automating a process involving filling out online forms on a web application. The process requires the user to upload a file from their computer to the web application. The company wants to automate this step using Blue Prism. Which of the following actions should be used in the Process layer to upload the file?

A) "Set Value" action

B) "Navigate" action

C) "Wait" action

D) "Attach" action

Explanation:

Answer - D

To upload a file to a web application, the "Attach" action should be used in the Process layer of Blue Prism. This action enables the robot to browse and select the file from the local machine and attach it to the web application. The "Set Value" action is used to set the value of a particular field, the "Navigate" action is used to navigate to a different page on the web application, and the "Wait" action is used to pause the robot for a specific amount of time.

Therefore, the correct answer is D.

Question 41:

A company is trying to automate data extraction from scanned PDF documents using Blue Prism. They want to know which OCR engine is used by Blue Prism for image recognition.

Which OCR engine is used by Blue Prism for image recognition?

A) Tesseract

B) Google Cloud Vision

C) ABBYY FineReader

D) OCR

Explanation:

Answer - A

The correct answer is A, Tesseract. Blue Prism uses OCR (Optical Character Recognition) technology to extract information from images, including scanned PDF documents. Tesseract is an open-source OCR engine that is commonly used by Blue Prism for image recognition. It has a high degree of accuracy and can reliably extract data from scanned images, provided they meet certain quality standards. While Blue Prism may be compatible with other OCR engines such as Google Cloud Vision or ABBYY FineReader, Tesseract is typically the default option.

Question 42:

As a Blue Prism developer, you are configuring a Login Agent to securely log into a client's system. You are aware that the Login Agent contains sensitive data, and you need to ensure that the resource PC follows the appropriate security policies. Which of the following security policies should you implement to protect the Login Agent's sensitive data?

A) Disable Ctrl+Alt+Del on the resource PC.

B) Remove the wallpaper on the resource PC.

C) Enable the lock screen immediately on the resource PC.

D) None of the above.

Explanation:

Answer - A

The correct response is choice A, which involves disabling Ctrl+Alt+Del on the resource PC. This step is crucial to ensure that the Login Agent can function correctly and securely without interference.

Choice B, which involves removing the wallpaper, is irrelevant to the security of the Login Agent and is therefore incorrect.

Choice C, which involves enabling the lock screen immediately on the resource PC, is also incorrect. While a lock screen is generally a good security practice, it may interfere with the Login Agent's functioning and is therefore not the best option in this scenario.

Choice D, which suggests that none of the above options are suitable, is incorrect since choice A is the best option for securing the Login Agent's sensitive data.

Therefore, the correct response is choice A, which involves disabling Ctrl+Alt+Del on the resource PC.

Question 43:

As a Blue Prism developer, you are responsible for managing user credentials and ensuring that they are properly administered. You need to know which access level is necessary to view user credentials in Blue Prism. Which of the following access levels is required to view user credentials?

A) Security - Manage Credentials permission.

B) Processes - Setup Authorizations.

C) Objects - Set Access Permissions.

D) Command Center.

Explanation:

Answer - A

The correct response is choice A, which requires the Security - Manage Credentials permission. This access level is necessary to access the Credentials tab in System Manager, where user credentials are managed.

Choice B, which involves Processes - Setup Authorizations, is incorrect. This access level is related to process setup and not user credential management.

Choice C, which involves Objects - Set Access Permissions, is also incorrect. This access level is related to object access permissions and not user credential management.

Choice D, which involves Command Center, is also incorrect. The configuration credentials are located in the System tab, not in the Command Center.

Therefore, the correct response is choice A, which requires the Security - Manage Credentials permission to view user credentials in Blue Prism.

Question 44:

As a Blue Prism developer, you are working on a project that involves retrieving the value of a specific property of a credential stored in Credential Manager. You need to know which action of the credentials Business object should be used to access that value and which property is stored by the Credential Manager. Which of the following actions of the credentials Business object should be used, and which property is stored by Credential Manager?

A) Read Property.

B) List Property.

C) Retrieve Property.

D) Get Property.

Explanation:

Answer - D

The correct response is choice D, which involves using the Get Property action to retrieve the value of a property of a credential stored in Credential Manager. The Credential Name and Property Name input parameters must be provided to perform this task.

Choices A, B, and C are incorrect because the credentials Business object does not support these operations.

Therefore, the correct response is choice D, which involves using the Get Property action to retrieve the value of a property of a credential stored in Credential Manager.

__Question 45:__

As a Blue Prism developer, you are configuring the Login Agent to add resource PCs from different domains. You need to know which configuration is best suited for adding computers from different domains as resource PCs. Which of the following configurations is best suited for this task?

A) Use the machine (short) name to register and the FQDN to interact.

B) Get a short name for your computer and start interacting with other machines.

C) To share data using the Machine Operating Unit, create an account.

D) None of the above.

Explanation:

Answer - A

The correct response is choice A, which involves registering the resource PCs using their fully qualified domain name (FQDN) and communicating using FQDNs. Blue Prism requires the use of FQDN when configuring multiple domain machines to ensure proper communication and functionality.

Choice B, which involves signing up for a machine short name and starting communication with other machines, is incorrect. This approach does not allow you to connect to machines in different domains using just the short name.

Choice C, which involves creating an account and exchanging data via the Machine Operating Unit, is also incorrect. Operating units are not utilized for machines and are not relevant to this scenario.

Choice D, which suggests that none of the above options are correct, is also incorrect. Since computers are registered using their FQDNs, option D is not a suitable answer.

Therefore, the correct response is choice A, which involves registering resource PCs using their FQDNs and communicating using FQDNs when configuring multiple domain machines.

Question 46:

As a Blue Prism developer, you are tasked with automating Citrix-hosted applications. You need to know the preferred approach to automating Citrix-hosted applications. Which of the following options is the best approach for automating Citrix-hosted applications?

A) Java Automation Tools.

B) Methods for Automating the Browser.

C) Techniques for Automating the Surface.

D) An Explanation of Citrix Automation.

Explanation:

Answer - C

Which involves using surface automation techniques to automate Citrix-hosted applications. Surface automation involves simulating user interaction with the graphical user interface (GUI) of an application. This approach is best suited for automating Citrix-hosted applications because they are typically presented as graphical images on the screen.

Choice A, which involves using Java Automation Tools, is incorrect because Java programs should be automated using Java automation techniques and are not relevant to automating Citrix-hosted applications.

Choice B, which involves using methods for automating the browser, is also incorrect. Browser automation is typically used for automating applications that run in a browser, whereas Citrix-hosted applications require a different approach.

Choice D, which involves providing an explanation of Citrix automation, is incorrect because Blue Prism does not support Citrix automation.

Therefore, the correct response is choice C, which involves using surface automation techniques to automate Citrix-hosted applications.

Question 47:

As a Blue Prism developer, you are working on a project that involves using the Regions action to read and recognize text and images. You need to know which option does not represent a reading stage of the

Regions action. Which of the following options is not a reading stage of the Regions action?

A) Read Text.

B) View an Image.

C) Recognize Text.

D) View a Picture.

Explanation:

Answer - D

The correct response is choice D, which does not represent a reading stage of the Regions action. While the Regions action can view images, it cannot recognize pictures. Blue Prism does not support the Recognize Pictures data function, so choice D is incorrect.

Choice A, which involves Read Text, is a reading stage of the Regions action. This stage involves extracting text from an image or screen area.

Choice B, which involves View an Image, is also a reading stage of the Regions action. This stage involves capturing an image from the screen and extracting information from it.

Choice C, which involves Recognize Text, is also a reading stage of the Regions action. This stage involves recognizing text using Optical Character Recognition (OCR) technology.

Therefore, the correct response is choice D, which does not represent a reading stage of the Regions action.

Question 48:

As a Blue Prism developer, you are tasked with implementing surface automation in a project. You need to know which tool is most commonly used for surface automation. Which of the following options is the most commonly used tool for surface automation?

A) Utility - General.

B) Utility - Image Manipulation.

C) Utility - Surface Automation.

D) Utility - Citrix.

Explanation:

Answer - B

The correct response is choice B, which involves using the Utility - Image Manipulation tool for surface automation. This tool is commonly used in Blue Prism for manipulating images and performing image recognition, which is essential for surface automation.

Choice A, which involves using the Utility - General tool, is incorrect because this tool is used for initiating operations, not surface automation.

Choice C, which involves using the Utility - Surface Automation tool, is also incorrect. This tool is not available in Blue Prism.

Choice D, which involves using the Utility - Citrix tool, is also incorrect because this tool is used for automating Citrix-based applications, not surface automation.

Therefore, the correct response is choice B, which involves using the Utility - Image Manipulation tool for surface automation.

Question 49:

As a Blue Prism developer, you are working on a project that involves extracting text from image files. You need to know which built-in Blue Prism feature uses the optical character recognition (OCR) method to decipher text in image files. Which of the following options is the correct built-in Blue Prism feature?

A) Read a Document with Optical Character Recognition Option.

B) Read a Document Option.

C) Read a Document (OCR).

Explanation:

Answer - A

The correct response is choice A, which involves using the Read a Document with Optical Character Recognition Option feature in Blue Prism to extract text from image files using OCR. This feature scans a window and extracts text from a rectangular area using OCR technology.

Choice B, which involves using the Read a Document Option feature, is incorrect because this feature only works inside a fixed window size and can only read text found using invasive methods.

Choice C, which involves using the Read a Document (OCR) feature, is also incorrect. Blue Prism does not support this feature.

Therefore, the correct response is choice A, which involves using the Read a Document with Optical Character Recognition Option feature in Blue Prism to extract text from image files using OCR.

Question 50:

As a Blue Prism developer, you are working on a project that involves extracting text from images using invasive techniques. You need to know which built-in Blue Prism feature is responsible for extracting text from images via the invasive technique. Which of the following options is the correct built-in Blue Prism feature?

A) Read a Document with Optical Character Recognition Option.

B) Read a Document Option.

C) Read a Document (OCR).

D) OCR (Optical Character Recognition).

Explanation:

Answer - B

The correct response is choice B, which involves using the Read a Document Option feature in Blue Prism to extract text from images via invasive techniques. This feature reads a specified rectangular window and extracts any text found within it using invasive techniques.

Choice A, which involves using the Read a Document with Optical Character Recognition Option feature, is incorrect because this feature uses OCR technology to extract text from images, not invasive techniques.

Choice C, which involves using the Read a Document (OCR) feature, is also incorrect because Blue Prism does not support this feature.

Choice D, which involves using the OCR (Optical Character Recognition) feature, is also incorrect because this is not a built-in Blue Prism feature.

Therefore, the correct response is choice B, which involves using the Read a Document Option feature in Blue Prism to extract text from images using invasive techniques.

Question 51:

As a Blue Prism developer, you are working on a project that involves using Tesseract for text extraction. You need to know how low of a value is needed for a certain level of sharpness. Which of the following options is the correct value?

A) 300 dots-per-inch.

B) 600 dots-per-inch.

C) 800 dots-per-inch.

D) 1200 dots-per-inch.

Explanation:

Answer - A

The correct response is choice A, which involves using a resolution of at least 300 dots-per-inch (dpi) for optimal recognition accuracy when using Tesseract for text extraction.

Choice B, which involves using a resolution of 600 dpi, is incorrect because a lower resolution of 300 dpi is sufficient for optimal recognition accuracy.

Choices C and D, which involve using resolutions of 800 and 1200 dpi, respectively, are also incorrect for the same reason. A resolution of 300 dpi is sufficient for optimal recognition accuracy when using Tesseract for text extraction.

Therefore, the correct response is choice A, which involves using a resolution of at least 300 dots-per-inch for optimal recognition accuracy when using Tesseract for text extraction.

Question 52:

As a Blue Prism developer, you are working on a project that involves surface automation. You need to know which feature of Windows needs to be turned off in order to make use of surface automation. Which of the following options is the correct feature?

A) Font Smoothing.

B) Bness.

C) Battery Power Options.

D) Screen Saver.

Explanation:

Answer - A

The correct response is choice A, which involves turning off the Font Smoothing feature in Windows to ensure that the OCR engine properly identifies characters for surface automation.

Choice B, which involves Bness, is incorrect because this is not a feature of Windows and does not impact surface automation.

Choice C, which involves Battery Power Options, is also incorrect because this feature does not significantly impact surface automation zones.

Choice D, which involves Screen Saver, is also incorrect because this feature does not affect surface automation.

Therefore, the correct response is choice A, which involves turning off the Font Smoothing feature in Windows to ensure optimal OCR recognition for surface automation.

Question 53:

As a Blue Prism developer, you are working on a project that involves advanced exception handling and task queues. You need to know the control room status that corresponds to the session after an unhandled exception causes the process to terminate. Which of the following options is the correct control room status?

A) Haltedly.

B) Stopped Instantly.

C) Completely Over.

D) Exception Has Been Canceled.

Explanation:

Answer - C

The correct response is choice C, which involves the status of Terminated in the control room when a process is halted due to an unhandled exception.

Choice A, which involves the Haltedly status, is incorrect because this is not a valid status in Blue Prism.

Choice B, which involves the Stopped Instantly status, is also incorrect because Blue Prism does not support an immediate paused status.

Choice D, which involves the Exception Has Been Canceled status, is also incorrect because this is not a valid status in Blue Prism.

Therefore, the correct response is choice C, which involves the Terminated status in the control room when a process is halted due to an unhandled exception.

Question 54:

As a Blue Prism developer, you are configuring a complex work queue with multiple tasks waiting to be completed. For a specific case with tags for "Work Type5" and "Customer Type10," but missing the "Branch Type 10" tag, how should the Get Next Item action be set up?

A) Add "+Work Type5; +Customer Type10; -Branch Type10" in the Tag Filter parameter.

B) Modify the Tag Filter parameter to read "Work Type5; Customer Type10; Branch Type10."

C) Modify the Tag Filter parameter to read "Work Type5, Customer Type10, Branch Type10."

D) Modify the Tag Filter parameter to read "-Work Type5; -Customer Type10; +Branch Type10."

Explanation:

Answer - A

Which involves adding "+Work Type5; +Customer Type10; -Branch Type10" in the Tag Filter parameter. This filters the task queue to retrieve the next item with the "Work Type5" and "Customer Type10" tags, but without the "Branch Type10" tag.

Choice B, which involves modifying the Tag Filter parameter to read "Work Type5; Customer Type10; Branch Type10," is incorrect because this retrieves items marked with all three tags, including the "Branch Type10" tag, which is not present in the case.

Choice C, which involves modifying the Tag Filter parameter to read "Work Type5, Customer Type10, Branch Type10," is also incorrect due to the syntax error. Tags should be separated by semicolons, not commas.

Choice D, which involves modifying the Tag Filter parameter to read "-Work Type5; -Customer Type10; +Branch Type10," is incorrect because it retrieves items without the "Work Type5" and "Customer Type10" tags, but with the "Branch Type10" tag, which is not present in the case.

Therefore, the correct response is choice A, which involves adding "+Work Type5; +Customer Type10; -Branch Type10" in the Tag Filter parameter to retrieve the next item with the "Work Type5" and "Customer Type10" tags, but without the "Branch Type10" tag.

Question 55:

A developer is designing a new business object in Blue Prism and is planning to include a large number of actions on a single page to accomplish a process module's goals. Which of the following statements is true regarding this approach?

A) Every action on the page should include a wait stage to prevent errors.

B) Blue Prism recommends having no more than 10 actions per page in Object Studio.

C) Business decisions should not be made within a business object's page design.

D) The design is flawless and can accommodate any number of actions.

Explanation:

Answer - C

It is not recommended to include business logic and decision-making within a business object's page design. This can complicate maintenance and change management, making it difficult to modify the process in the future. Option A is not entirely accurate because wait stages should only be used when necessary to prevent errors or timing issues. Option B is not correct as there is no set limit on the number of actions per page, but it is recommended to keep pages with minimal actions for ease of maintenance. Option D is not true as even the best-designed page can become complicated and challenging to maintain over time.

Question 56:

A company uses Blue Prism's work queues to manage customer service requests. The company receives a large number of requests each day, and they need a system that prioritizes requests in the order they are received. Which approach does Blue Prism work queues use to handle these work cases?

A) Last-in, first-out (LIFO)

B) First-in, first-out (FIFO)

C) Today First

D) Day of the Future First

Explanation:

Answer - B

First-in, first-out (FIFO). Blue Prism's work queues follow a FIFO approach by default, which means that the first request received will be the first to be processed. This is the most suitable approach for the given scenario where the company wants to prioritize requests based on the order they are received.

Option A, Last-in, first-out (LIFO), is not applicable here as it would prioritize the newest requests over the older ones, which is not what the company wants.

Option C, Today First, prioritizes the requests received on the current day over the older ones. This approach is not suitable for the scenario described as it doesn't follow the order in which the requests were received.

Option D, Day of the Future First, prioritizes requests based on the date they need to be completed in the future. This approach is not suitable for the given scenario as the company wants to prioritize requests based on the order they are received.

Question 57:

A healthcare organization is using Blue Prism's work queues to manage patient appointments. The organization has three types of appointments: urgent, routine, and follow-up. Urgent appointments are the highest priority, followed by routine appointments, and then follow-up appointments. Which of the following statements is true for retrieving the next case item from the queue?

A) Lowest Priority number first

B) Highest Priority number first

C) Negative Priority number first

D) Decimal Priority number first

Explanation:

Answer - A

Get Next Item selects items in order of the lowest Priority number first. In this scenario, the healthcare organization has assigned priority numbers to each type of appointment, with urgent being the highest priority and follow-up being the lowest. Therefore, when retrieving the next case item from the queue, Blue Prism will prioritize the appointment with the lowest priority number first, which in this case is an urgent appointment.

Option B, Get Next Item selects items in order of the highest Priority number first, is incorrect as the organization has assigned higher priority numbers to lower priority appointments.

Option C, Get Next Item selects items in order of the negative Priority number first, and Option D, Get Next Item selects items in order of the decimal Priority number first, are both incorrect as the organization has not used negative or decimal numbers to assign priorities to the appointments.

Therefore, option A is the correct response for this scenario.

Question 58:

A financial institution uses Blue Prism to process loan applications. During the loan processing, the system encounters various exceptions, such as missing documents or incorrect information. Which of the following options does not involve the use of an exception?

A) ExceptionText()

B) ExceptionDetail()

C) ExceptionStage()

D) ExceptionTypes()

Explanation:

Answer - D

The correct answer is option D, ExceptionTypes(). Blue Prism includes the ExceptionText(), ExceptionDetail(), and ExceptionStage() functions to handle exceptions during a process. ExceptionText() is used to retrieve the text description of the last exception that occurred, while ExceptionDetail() provides a detailed description of the last exception. ExceptionStage() is used to retrieve the stage name where the last exception occurred.

Option A, ExceptionText(), and Option B, ExceptionDetail(), are both incorrect because they are functions used to handle exceptions in Blue Prism. ExceptionText() is used to retrieve the text description of the last exception that occurred, and ExceptionDetail() provides a detailed description of the last exception.

Option C, ExceptionStage(), is also incorrect because it is a function used to handle exceptions in Blue Prism. ExceptionStage() is used to retrieve the stage name where the last exception occurred.

Therefore, option D, ExceptionTypes(), is the correct response as it is not a function used to handle exceptions in Blue Prism.

Question 59:

A retail company uses Blue Prism to manage their inventory system. During the inventory update process, the system encounters various exceptions, such as system exceptions, exceptions to the rule in business procedures, and exceptions occurring due to invalid input. Which kind of exceptions is amenable to modification?

A) System Exceptions

B) Exceptions to the Rule in Business Procedures

C) Exceptions Occurring Due to Invalid Input

D) There should not be any alterations made to the rule of no.

Explanation:

Answer - A

System Exceptions. System exceptions are errors that occur in the target system during the automation process. These exceptions can be modified in real-time by making changes to the integration of the target system with Blue Prism. Once the target system is restarted, the exception should go away.

Option B, Exceptions to the Rule in Business Procedures, is incorrect as these exceptions are typically caused by an unexpected user action that does not follow the predefined business procedures. These exceptions cannot be modified, and manual intervention from the user is required to resolve the issue.

Option C, Exceptions Occurring Due to Invalid Input, is also incorrect as these exceptions occur when the system receives invalid input, such as incorrect data or format. These exceptions cannot be modified, and the system needs to communicate the error to the user.

Option D, there should not be any alterations made to the rule of no, is incorrect as system exceptions can be modified by making changes to the integration of the target system with Blue Prism.

Therefore, option A is the correct response in this scenario.

Question 60:

A manufacturing company uses Blue Prism to process purchase orders received via email. Each email can contain hundreds of purchase orders in its body, and the company wants to automate the process of adding each purchase order as a separate item to the Work Queue. Which of the following statements is correct?

A) There should be a separate dedicated task queue for each incoming email.

B) Using the same value in the get next item action, a case item can be retrieved after being labelled with the topic line and sender's name.

C) Emails sent to different mailboxes should trigger various robots with independent task queues.

D) There is no way to automate this with Blue Prism.

Explanation:

Answer - B

A case item can be labelled with the subject line and sender's name, and then retrieved using the same value in the get next item action. Blue Prism allows case items to be labelled with various tags, such as the subject line and sender's name, which can be used to retrieve the case item using the same value in the Get Next Item action. This approach will allow each purchase order in the email body to be added as a separate item to the Work Queue.

Option A, each incoming email should have its own dedicated work queue, is incorrect as the Blue Prism process cannot dynamically know which queues to use. Creating a dedicated work queue for each incoming email can lead to a large number of queues that are difficult to manage.

Option C, Multiple robots with separate task queues should be activated by emails sent to separate mailboxes, is also incorrect as this approach requires multiple robots with separate task queues to be activated by emails sent to separate mailboxes. This can be costly and requires additional licensing and infrastructure.

Option D, there is no way to automate this with Blue Prism, is incorrect as Blue Prism provides a means to automate such processes.

Therefore, option B is the correct response in this scenario.

Question 61:

A transportation company is using Blue Prism to automate their freight shipping process. One of the pages in the process is configured to have two recover stages without using an exception block. Which of the following is a difficulty in the page design?

A) There shouldn't be two recover phases on a page.

B) No more than one resume step should be present on each page.

C) Use the Exception Block in the Page.

D) Numerous recoveries or resume steps on a single screen are superfluous.

Explanation:

Answer - D

The correct response is option D, It is unnecessary to have many recoveries or resume steps on one page. While it is possible for a page to have multiple recover stages without using an exception block, having too many recoveries or resume steps on one page can make the page design overly complex and difficult to manage.

Option A, A page should not have two recover stages, is incorrect as a page can have multiple recover stages, and it is a valid design choice in certain situations.

Option B, there should not be more than one resume stage per page, is also incorrect as a page can have multiple resume stages, and it is a valid design choice in certain situations.

Option C, Exception Block should be utilised in a Page, is incorrect as a page can be designed without an exception block, and it is a valid design choice in certain situations.

Therefore, option D is the correct response in this scenario. While having multiple recover stages without using an exception block is possible, it can make the page design overly complex, and it is unnecessary to have many recoveries or resume steps on one page.

Question 62:

A logistics company is using Blue Prism to automate their shipping process. One of the pages in the process is configured to have two recover stages without using an exception block. If an error occurs at the Launch traverse stage, which recovery strategy would be implemented?

A) Page will execute successfully if you select the recover1 route.

B) If Page chooses the recover2 path, it will become trapped in an endless cycle.

C) Due to the absence of an exception block, the page will generate an error.

D) Not any of the above

Explanation:

Answer - A

Choosing recover1 path will result in a successful execution of Page. When an error occurs at the Launch traverse stage, the recovery strategy implemented would be to choose recover1 path. This will allow the process to continue and complete successfully, without the need for an exception block or multiple recover stages.

Option B, If Page takes the recover2 route, it will get stuck in a never-ending loop, is incorrect as the recover2 route does not lead to an infinite loop.

Option C, Page will throw an error since there is no Exception Block, is also incorrect as a page can be designed without an exception block, and it is a valid design choice in certain situations.

Therefore, option A is the correct response in this scenario. The recover1 path will catch and process any errors that occur at the Launch traverse stage, and the process will continue successfully.

Question 63:

A finance company is using Blue Prism to automate their invoice processing. Which of the following options does NOT represent an internal exception in this scenario?

A) The choice in this instance was not a yes-or-no one because

B) the user was already logged into a program

C) the option was not immediately apparent.

D) Invalid validation

Explanation:

Answer - D

The correct response is option D, Invalid validation. Invalid validation is an example of an external exception that occurs when the input data is not valid or does not meet the validation criteria. It is not an internal exception.

Option A, In this case, the decision was not a yes/no one because, is an example of an internal exception that occurs when a decision cannot be made based on the input data.

Option B, the user was already logged into a program, is also an example of an internal exception that occurs when a user is already logged into a program, and the automation process cannot log in again.

Option C, the option was not immediately apparent, is another example of an internal exception that occurs when an option is not immediately clear or available based on the input data.

Therefore, option D is the correct response in this scenario. Invalid validation is not an internal exception but an external one that occurs during the validation process.

Question 64:

A retail company is using Blue Prism to automate their inventory management. Which of the following phrases best describes the robot's choice to try again in the event of internal and external failures?

A) [Number of Attempts] Lower(ExceptionType())="system exception" OR Lower(ExceptionType())="internal" AND [Retry Limit] Retry Attempts >

B) [Maximum Attempts] Lower(ExceptionType()) = "system exception" OR Lower(ExceptionType()) = "internal".

C) [Attempts to Retry] Retry Attempts Allowed: Conversely, AND (Lower(ExceptionType())> System error OR internal error as determined by Lower(ExceptionType()).

D) [Attempt Count] Retry Attempts Bounded By: ([Retry Limit] AND (Lower(ExceptionType())="system exception" OR Lower(ExceptionType())> "internal")

Explanation:

Answer - A

The correct response is option A, [Number of Attempts] Lower(ExceptionType())="system exception" OR Lower(ExceptionType())="internal" AND [Retry Limit] Retry Attempts >. This expression represents the correct Retry decision for the robot to attempt again in case of internal and external failures. If the Retry Count has not been reached and the exception type is either a System Exception or an Internal Exception, then the flow will retry.

Option B, [Maximum Attempts] Lower(ExceptionType()) = "system exception" OR Lower(ExceptionType()) = "internal", is incorrect as it does not specify the Retry Count or the Retry Limit.

Option C, [Attempts to Retry] Retry Attempts Allowed: Conversely, AND (Lower(ExceptionType())> System error OR internal error as determined by Lower(ExceptionType()), is also incorrect as it does not specify the Retry Count or the Retry Limit.

Option D, [Attempt Count] Retry Attempts Bounded By: ([Retry Limit] AND (Lower(ExceptionType())="system exception" OR Lower(ExceptionType())> "internal"), is incorrect as it specifies that the flow will only retry if the Retry Count has not been reached and if the exception type is neither a System Exception nor an Internal Exception, which is not what is required.

Therefore, option A is the correct response in this scenario, as it specifies the correct conditions for the flow to retry in case of internal and external failures.

Question 65:

A logistics company is using Blue Prism to automate their order processing. Where can they find a list of all the various exception types used by various business objects and procedures in Blue Prism?

A) Control Room

B) Exception Studio

C) Exception Detail

D) System

Explanation:

Answer - D

The correct response is option D, System. The System page in Blue Prism allows users to view a list of all the different exception types being used by different business objects and processes. It provides an overview of all the available exceptions, their types, and how they are used in the business processes.

Option A, Control Room, is incorrect as it is primarily used to monitor robot performance and manage resources.

Option B, Exception Studio, is also incorrect as there is no such feature in Blue Prism.

Option C, Exception Detail, is not relevant to this question as it refers to a specific feature used to provide details about an exception that has occurred during a process.

Therefore, option D is the correct response in this scenario, as it provides the information required to view a list of all the different exception types being used in Blue Prism.

Question 66:

A manufacturing company is using Blue Prism to automate their production line. Among the options given, to what does the process exception NOT occur?

A) A calculation that uses a bad phrase.

B) "Press" an imaginary button.

C) Unexpected break in the schedule.

D) Two last steps on the same page.

Explanation:

Answer - D

Two last steps on the same page. A process exception can occur due to any of the other options given. For example, an invalid expression can cause a computation exception, pressing an imaginary button can cause a runtime exception, and an unanticipated pause in the program can cause a system exception.

Option D, however, is not a cause of a process exception. While having two last steps on the same page may result in an error or issue with the automation process, it is not a cause of a process exception specifically.

Therefore, option D is the correct response in this scenario, as it is the only option that does not refer to a cause of a process exception.

Question 67:

A company is using Blue Prism to manage their job queues. How can they change the retry settings for items in a queue?

A) Command Center

B) Production Studio

C) Monitoring Center

D) Manager of Systems

Explanation:

Answer - D

The correct response is option D, Manager of Systems. The Blue Prism System Manager module is used to modify the retry settings for items in a job queue. This module provides a range of system management tools, including the ability to change the retry settings for queued items.

Option A, Command Center, is incorrect as it is primarily used for monitoring the day-to-day operations and managing schedules.

Option B, Production Studio, is also incorrect as it is used for designing processes that incorporate business logic and rules.

Option C, Monitoring Center, is not relevant to this question as it is not a feature of Blue Prism.

Therefore, option D is the correct response in this scenario, as it provides the information required to change the retry settings for items in a job queue.

Question 68:

Complex Exception Handling and Job Queuing

When running the process, the error "Internal: stack imbalance has reached" occurred.

Is there any way to explain this unusual occurrence?

A) It's a new Exception and the process or business object was already in Exception mode.

B) The final step of the process was run while it was in recovery.

C) 100 mistakes have occurred in the process.

D) There was no page that used the recover stage.

Explanation:

Answer - B

Option B is the correct response.

Choice A is not accurate since a process will be terminated with a second exception if it encounters an exception while in recover mode.

For this reason, Option B is the right answer: if the end stage is executed while the process is in the recover stage, a stack imbalance error will occur.

Stack imbalance exceptions are not brought on by process faults, hence choice C is not valid.

Due to the process being aborted at the lack of a recover stage, choice D is incorrect.

Question 69:

A business process involves a complex page that performs various actions and calculations. However, there may be instances where exceptions occur during the page execution, such as when the system is unable to retrieve necessary data. To handle these exceptions, the page needs to be enclosed in a stage that can catch and handle them appropriately.

What stage is used to enclose the page exceptions in the above scenario?

A) Blocking

B) Handling Exceptions

C) Recovering Data

D) Resuming Normal

E. Operations

Explanation:

Answer - A

The correct answer is A. The blocking stage is used to enclose the page and catch any exceptions that occur during its execution. This allows the flow to continue even if an exception is encountered. Option B is incorrect since the handling exceptions stage is used to specify how different types of exceptions are handled, rather than enclosing the page itself. Option C is also incorrect since the recovering data stage is used to recover data lost due to an exception. Option D is not relevant in this scenario, as it pertains to resuming the flow after an exception has been handled. Finally, option E is not related to exception handling and is therefore incorrect.

Question 70:

A Blue Prism developer is reviewing a queue case in the production environment and notices that there is an exception marked but no exception details are provided. The developer investigates the issue to determine the possible explanation.

What could account for an exception noted in the queue but without any associated exception details?

A) The unhandled exception stage's attributes are empty.

B) It's a bug in Blue Prism's internal code.

C) Process shutdown due to private exception.

D) Implementation of the preserve check done incorrectly.

Explanation:

Answer - A

The correct answer is A, which means that leaving the properties of an exception stage blank will trigger an empty exception. Therefore, the developer should fill in the properties of the unhandled exception stage to provide exception details.

Option B is not a valid explanation because the issue is not caused by a bug in Blue Prism's internal code.

Option C is not the correct explanation because if the process had terminated with an internal exception, there would be some exception details provided in the queue case.

Option D is also not the correct explanation because using the preserve check to rethrow the exception disqualifies it.

In conclusion, the most likely explanation for the exception marked in the queue case without any exception details provided is that the properties of the unhandled exception stage are unfilled.

Question 71:

A software developer is seeking guidance from Blue Prism on best practices for object layer layout in software development.

What does Blue Prism suggest for object layer layout?

A) Every screen in the application ought to reflect a different piece of business data.

B) Each step of the procedure ought to have its own business object.

C) A Single Business Object to Support All Tasks

D) None of the above

Explanation:

Answer - A

The correct answer is A, which means that when designing an application, each screen should represent a unique business object.

Option A is the best practice recommended by Blue Prism as each screen's business object can be reused in other procedures. It also ensures that each time an update is made to the object layer, the risk to the underlying process layer is minimal.

Option B is not the correct answer because although it uses the same application page, the task's business object cannot be reused.

Option C is also not the correct answer because having a single business object to support all tasks poses a significant threat to the underlying process layer.

In conclusion, it is best practice to have one business object per screen when designing an application, according to Blue Prism's recommendation.

Question 72:

A software developer is reviewing the commands "Request Stop" and "Immediate Stop" in Blue Prism and wants to understand the distinction between them.

What characterizes the distinction between the commands "Request Stop" and "Immediate Stop"?

A) "Immediate stop" stops a procedure immediately, whereas "request stop" stops it gradually.

B) Both "request stop" and "immediate stop" halt a process, but "request stop" does it on the resource PC while "immediate stop" does it on the interactive client machine.

C) Request stop does nothing in the lack of an IsStopRequested() function check in the process, whereas "immediate stop" ends the process whether or not the check is executed.

D) "Request Stop" and "Immediate Stop" mean the same thing.

Explanation:

Answer - C

The correct answer is C, which means that in the absence of an IsStopRequested() function check in the process, "Request Stop" does nothing, whereas "Immediate Stop" terminates the process whether or not the check is implemented.

Option A is not the correct answer because "Request Stop" and "Immediate Stop" both bring the process to a halt abruptly.

Option B is also not the correct answer because it suggests that "Request Stop" terminates processes on the resource PC while "Immediate Stop" does so on the interactive client machine, which is not true.

Option D is not the correct answer because "Request Stop" and "Immediate Stop" have different meanings and functions.

In conclusion, "Request Stop" and "Immediate Stop" are two distinct commands in Blue Prism. "Request Stop" updates the session variable "StopRequested" and requires the worker process to periodically query the IsStopRequested() method to ensure a smooth shutdown. On the other hand, "Immediate Stop" terminates the current action and marks the present queue case as an exception, causing the execution to cease immediately.

Question 73:

A Blue Prism developer needs to verify the web services for their project and is presented with several URLs as options.

Which URL can be used to verify the Blue Prism web services?

A) This machine is the Blue Prism resource port, and its URL is: http://[machinename]:[ws/].

B) http://[machinename]/ws/

C) The format is http://[hostname]:[port]/[program name].

D) http://[machinename]:[port]/ws/[ObjectName]

Explanation:

Answer - A

The correct answer is A, which means that the Blue Prism web services can be verified via the WSDL, which is available at the following URL: http://[machinename]:[ws/].

Option B is not the correct answer because it only provides the hostname and "/ws/" but doesn't specify the port number.

Option C is not the correct answer because it is a generic format for a URL and does not provide any specific information about the Blue Prism web services.

Option D is also not the correct answer because it provides the hostname, port number, and object name, but does not include "/ws/" in the URL.

In conclusion, the Blue Prism developer can verify the web services for their project using the URL http://[machinename]:[ws/], where the machinename is the name of the computer where Blue Prism's resource port is located, and ws is the default port for Blue Prism web services.

Question 74:

A Blue Prism developer is looking for the user interface to set up native interfaces with systems and services that have made their HTTP APIs publicly available.

Which part of the system tab includes a user interface for setting up native interfaces with systems and services that have made their HTTP APIs publicly available?

A) Methods for Managing Competencies

B) Web services that use the Simple Object Access Protocol (SOAP)

C) Api Web

D) None

Explanation:

Answer - C

The correct answer is C, which means that the "Api Web" section of the system tab includes a user interface for setting up native interfaces with systems and services that have made their HTTP APIs publicly available.

Option A is not the correct answer because the "Methods for Managing Competencies" section of the system tab is used to configure connectors for third-party applications, not HTTP APIs.

Option B is also not the correct answer because it refers to setting up web services that use the Simple Object Access Protocol (SOAP), which is a different type of web service protocol.

Option D is not the correct answer because the user interface for setting up native interfaces with systems and services that have made their HTTP APIs publicly available is provided by the "Api Web" section.

In conclusion, to configure HTTP web APIs in Blue Prism, a developer would use the user interface provided by the "Api Web" section of the system tab. This functionality allows for native interactions with systems and services that have published HTTP APIs, such as RESTful Web Services.

Question 75:

A Blue Prism developer needs to interface with a COM (Component Object Models) object in a Windows context and is presented with several options.

In a Windows context, which level is often used to interface with a COM object?

A) Coding Phase

B) The Middle of the Action

C) Page

D) Subprocess Phase

Explanation:

Answer - A

The correct answer is A, which means that the coding phase is often used to interface with a COM object in a Windows context.

Option B is not the correct answer because it suggests that the middle of the action is where a COM object is typically interfaced with, but this is not the case.

Option C is also not the correct answer because the page stage is used to invoke a different page of the same business object, not to interface with a COM object.

Option D is not the correct answer because the subprocess step is used to invoke another process, not to interface with a COM object.

In conclusion, when interfacing with a COM object in a Windows context, a developer would typically use the coding phase in Blue Prism. The coding phase is where the developer can write and execute custom code to interact with the COM object.

Question 76:

A Blue Prism developer needs to register a web service and is presented with several command line options.

Which command line with the automate switch should be used to register a web service in Blue Prism?

A) /regwebservice

B) /addwebservice

C) /exposewebservice

D) /modwebservice

Explanation:

Answer - A

The correct answer is A, which means that the /regwebservice command with the automate switch can be used to register a web service in Blue Prism.

Option B is not the correct answer because there is no /addwebservice command in Blue Prism.

Option C is also not the correct answer because there is no /exposewebservice command in Blue Prism.

Option D is not the correct answer because there is no /modwebservice command in Blue Prism.

In conclusion, to register a web service in Blue Prism, a developer should use the /regwebservice command with the automate switch on the command line. This command allows the developer to register a web service in Blue Prism and integrate it into their project.

Question 77:

A Blue Prism developer needs to find the .NET data type that most closely matches Blue Prism's flag data type.

Which .NET data type is most similar to Blue Prism's flag data type?

A) Boolean

B) Char

C) String

D) Bit

Explanation:

Answer - A

The correct answer is A, which means that the Boolean data type in .NET is most similar to Blue Prism's flag data type.

Option B is not the correct answer because the Char data type in .NET is not equivalent to Blue Prism's flag data type.

Option C is also not the correct answer because the String data type in .NET is not equivalent to Blue Prism's flag data type.

Option D is not the correct answer because although the Bit data type in .NET is similar to Blue Prism's Bit data type, it is not equivalent to Blue Prism's flag data type.

In conclusion, when working with Blue Prism's flag data type, a developer can use the Boolean data type in .NET as the closest equivalent. Blue Prism's flag data type maps 1:1 to the Boolean data type in .NET.

Question 78:

A Blue Prism developer needs to map complicated data types when connecting to other web services and is presented with several options.

Which data type from Blue Prism is used to map complicated data types when connecting to other web services?

A) Numbers

B) Collections

C) Strings

D) List

Explanation:

Answer - B

The correct answer is B, which means that Collections are used in Blue Prism to map complicated data types when connecting to other web services.

Option A is not the correct answer because Numbers are used to map simple numeric data types such as int, float, decimal, etc. and not complicated data types.

Option C is also not the correct answer because Strings are used to map string data types and not complicated data types.

Option D is not the correct answer because Blue Prism does not support the List data type.

In conclusion, when working with complicated data types from other web services in Blue Prism, a developer should use Collections to map these data types. Collections are used to store complicated data types and allow for easy mapping of these data types to Blue Prism's data types.

Question 79:

A Blue Prism developer is configuring auto-initialization for connecting to a Business Object and is presented with several options.

How many sessions are established in a resource machine when connecting to a Business Object via auto-initialization?

A) 0

B) 1

C) The total number of vulnerable business objects

D) Connected call count

Explanation:

Answer - B

The correct answer is B, which means that only one session is established in a resource machine when connecting to a Business Object via auto-initialization.

Option A is not the correct answer because a license is required to use a Business Object, and once the connection is configured to auto-initialize, a session is established automatically.

Option C is also not the correct answer because auto-initialization allows for a single instance of a Business Object, so the total number of vulnerable Business Objects is not relevant to the number of sessions established.

Option D is not the correct answer because the number of connected calls is not relevant to the number of sessions established in a resource machine when connecting to a Business Object via auto-initialization.

In conclusion, when connecting to a Business Object via auto-initialization, Blue Prism automatically establishes a single session in the resource machine. This allows requests to accessible Business Objects to be automatically assigned to the session, allowing for the use of object services.

Question 80:

A Blue Prism developer needs to establish three simultaneous auto-initialized connections to three "Exclusive" run mode Business Objects that are available as web services.

How many client machines (PCs) are required to set up three Business Objects connections that are simultaneously auto-initialized?

A) 0

B) 1

C) 3

D) Equal amount of calls

Explanation:

Answer - C

The correct answer is C, which means that three client computers (PCs) are needed to establish three simultaneous auto-initialized connections to Business Objects.

Option A is not the correct answer because a license is required to access a Business Object, and therefore a client computer (PC) is needed.

Option B is also not the correct answer because using a specialized Business Object requires a number of licenses proportional to the number of objects being used.

Option D is not the correct answer because the number of calls is not relevant to the number of client computers (PCs) needed to establish the connections.

In conclusion, in order to establish three simultaneous auto-initialized connections to three "Exclusive" run mode Business Objects, a developer would need three client computers (PCs). This is because exclusive run mode Business Objects require a dedicated license and resource PC for each instance, so one resource PC cannot be used for multiple connections.

Question 81:

A Blue Prism developer needs to manually initialize a connection to a Business Object and is presented with several options.

How many sessions are produced when manually initializing a connection to a Business Object?

A) 0

B) 1

C) Calls for service are almost even in number

D) It's not any of the aforementioned

Explanation:

Answer - B

The correct answer is B, which means that when manually initializing a connection to a Business Object, one session is produced.

Option A is not the correct answer because a license is required to access a Business Object, and once a connection is manually initialized, at least one session is established.

Option C is not the correct answer because the number of calls is not relevant to the number of sessions established when manually initializing a connection to a Business Object. Each caller is responsible for managing the session creation in their own code.

Option D is not the correct answer because a session is established when manually initializing a connection to a Business Object.

In conclusion, when manually initializing a connection to a Business Object, a developer will establish at least one session. Each caller is responsible for managing the session creation in their own code, and typically, a caller will initiate a session to manage multiple calls at once.

Question 82:

A Blue Prism developer is running Process A in Foreground mode on Machine1 when five web service requests are received in rapid succession, all of which are destined for the currently active Process B.

What is the possible outcome in this scenario?

A) Process A will be halted while Process B is given access to the machine.

B) On Machine1, five separate sessions will start up.

C) There will be six new sessions on Machine1.

D) Five web service calls will be refused with this session.

Explanation:

Answer - D

The correct answer is D, which means that five web service calls will be refused with this session.

Option A is not the correct answer because the active session is required for the execution of Process A, and therefore, Process A will not be halted while Process B is given access to the machine.

Option B is not the correct answer because the machine will not initiate a session for each web service request.

Option C is not the correct answer because it is not possible to create a Foreground session of the same kind when it is ready to display.

In conclusion, the possible outcome in this scenario is that five web service calls will be refused with this session. When a foreground process is running, it holds the active session, and other processes cannot access the same session until it is released. Therefore, the web service requests destined for Process B will not be processed until the session is released by Process A.

Question 83:

As a Blue Prism developer, you have developed an automation process that opens Internet Explorer with multiple tabs to perform a series of tasks. When you check the task management window, you notice that there are multiple processes with the name "iexplorer" running. Which of the following options best describes the current situation?

A) The automation process was designed to launch several instances of IE within the web app.

B) Blue Prism launched multiple separate instances of Internet Explorer to perform the tasks.

C) Each tab in Internet Explorer is running as a distinct process.

D) None of the above options describes the current situation.

Explanation:

Answer - C

In this scenario, the multiple instances of "iexplorer" in the task management window indicate that each tab in Internet Explorer is running as a distinct process. This is because each session of Internet Explorer is executed in its own child Windows process that is generated from the parent process. Each session has its own unique index, based on the chronological sequence in which the session's corresponding process was initially formed. The attach action of a navigate stage is where the Child Index is set. Therefore, option C is the best choice. Options A and B are incorrect because they suggest that the automation process or Blue Prism launched the multiple instances of IE, which is not the case. Option D is incorrect because there is a clear explanation for the situation, which is that each tab in Internet Explorer is running as a distinct process.

Question 84:

As a Blue Prism developer, you are tasked with establishing interprocess communication between two applications running on Microsoft Windows using Blue Prism. Which of the following application modeller elements should you use?

A) DDE Component

B) Tags in Hypertext Markup Language (HTML)

C) AA Constituents

D) Win32 Components

.

Explanation:

Answer - A

In order to establish interprocess communication between two applications on Microsoft Windows using Blue Prism, the best option is to use the Dynamic Data Exchange (DDE) component. DDE is a technique for transferring information between computer programs, making it a suitable option for this scenario. Therefore, option A is the correct choice.

Option B, which suggests using tags in HTML, is incorrect because HTML is primarily used for creating web pages and does not provide a way to establish interprocess communication.

Option C, which suggests using AA constituents, is also incorrect. AA (ActiveAction) elements are used for interacting with Windows applications, not for interprocess communication.

Option D, which suggests using Win32 components, is also incorrect. Win32 components are used for low-level interaction with Windows operating systems, but they are not the best option for establishing interprocess communication between two applications. Therefore, option A (DDE Component) is the best choice for this scenario.

Question 85:

As a Blue Prism developer, you are automating a web page and you need to ensure that the page and all of its child frames are fully loaded before performing certain actions. Which of the following options should you use as a placeholder until the website finishes loading?

A) File Uploaded

B) Parental Document

C) Verify Existence of Page

D) Verify the Existence.

Explanation:

Answer - B

The correct option to use as a placeholder until the website finishes loading in this scenario is the Parental Document. This is because waiting for a page and all of its child frames to finish loading is a mandatory condition for some actions, and the Parental Document verifies both the existence of the element and the completion of loading for the entire page and all of its child frames. Therefore, option B is the correct choice.

Option A, which suggests using File Uploaded, is incorrect because it is not related to waiting for a web page to load.

Option C, which suggests using Verify Existence of Page, is also incorrect. Blue Prism does not have a feature called "Check Page Exist," so this option is not valid.

Option D, which suggests using Verify the Existence, is also incorrect because it only cares about whether or not the provided element is present on the page, and does not check if the page and its child frames have finished loading. Therefore, option B (Parental Document) is the best choice in this scenario.

Question 86:

As a Blue Prism developer, you are trying to automate a Silverlight application, but you are facing difficulties due to the way the application is presented as a windowless plug-in. Which of the following properties must be set to false in order to automate the Silverlight application more easily?

A) Building without any windows

B) Property of Active Accessibility

C) Windows 32-bit system variables

D) None of the above

Explanation:

Answer - A

To easily automate Silverlight applications, the windowless attribute should be set to false. This is because the feature that allows Silverlight programs to be presented as a windowless plug-in is typically set to true, which makes it difficult to automate the application. By setting the windowless attribute to false, you can enable automation of Silverlight applications more easily. Therefore, option A is the correct choice.

Option B, which suggests the property of Active Accessibility, is incorrect because Blue Prism does not have this characteristic.

Option C, which suggests using Windows 32-bit system variables, is also incorrect because this option is not supported in Blue Prism.

Option D, which suggests that none of the above options are correct, is incorrect because option A is the correct choice. Therefore, option A (Building without any windows) is the best choice for this scenario.

Question 87:

As a Blue Prism developer, you are trying to locate ActiveX components in a destination browser to automate certain actions. In which mode should the ActiveX components be located in the destination browser?

A) Accessibility Activation (AA) Mode

B) Mode Win32

C) HTML Compatibility Mode

D) Surface Automated Processing

Explanation:

Answer - D

The best mode for locating and automating ActiveX components in a destination browser is Surface Automated Processing. This is because using Surface Automation techniques is the best approach for automating any ActiveX components present in the target browser program. Therefore, option D is the correct choice.

Option A, which suggests using Accessibility Activation (AA) mode, is incorrect because ActiveX components cannot be spied in AA mode.

Option B, which suggests using Win32 mode, is also incorrect due to technical limitations. Win32 mode cannot eavesdrop on ActiveX components.

Option C, which suggests using HTML Compatibility mode, is also incorrect because HTML mode cannot inspect ActiveX components stealthily. Therefore, options A and C are ruled out, and option D (Surface Automated Processing) is the best choice for this scenario.

Question 88:

As a Blue Prism developer, you are running a process that operates on a mainframe application, but an error occurs at launch with the following message: "Error loading dynamic link library (DLL): 'HLLAPI32.DLL' not found." What is the cause of this error?

A) The mainframe programme is not installed on the computer.

B) A new computer that is not yet accessible through Blue Prism.

C) The Windows PATH environment variable does not contain the mainframe installation path.

D) A Resource PC cannot access mainframe software in any manner.

Explanation:

Answer - C

The error message "Error loading dynamic link library (DLL): 'HLLAPI32.DLL' not found" typically appears when a mainframe application is launched. This error occurs because the directory where the mainframe software was installed is not included in the Windows PATH environment variable. Therefore, the correct option is C, which states that the mainframe installation directory is not included in the Windows PATH environment variable.

Option A, which suggests that the computer does not have the mainframe software loaded, is incorrect because the error message specifically mentions the DLL file not being found.

Option B, which suggests a brand-new mainframe that is not currently available through Blue Prism, is also incorrect because it is not related to the error message.

Option D, which suggests that there is no way to use a Resource PC to access mainframe software, is also incorrect because it is not related to the error message. Therefore, option C (the mainframe installation directory is not included in the Windows PATH environment variable) is the best choice for this scenario.

Question 89:

As a Blue Prism developer, you are integrating in "Embedded" mode and need to know which version of Java should be used on the target system. Which version of Java should be used?

A) 64-bit

B) 32-bit

C) Either of these

D) None of the above

Explanation:

Answer - B

When integrating in "Embedded" mode, the correct version of Java to use on the target system is the 32-bit version. This is because "Embedded" mode is used for Business Objects that mimic 32-bit Java programs. Therefore, option B is the correct choice.

Option A, which suggests using the 64-bit version of Java, is incorrect because a 32-bit version of Java must be installed to use "Embedded" mode.

Option C, which suggests that either the 64-bit or 32-bit version of Java can be used, is also incorrect because only the 32-bit version is suitable for "Embedded" mode.

Option D, which suggests that none of the above options are correct, is also incorrect because the 32-bit version of Java should be used in "Embedded" mode. Therefore, option B (32-bit) is the best choice for this scenario.

Question 90:

As a Blue Prism developer, you are attempting to automate a Java-based application. However, the application does not allow any kind of eavesdropping. In this scenario, which feature of the application modeller should you use for scanning?

A) Application Navigator

B) The DDE elements

C) HTC components

D) Diagnostics

Explanation:

Answer - A

When automating a Java-based application that does not allow any kind of eavesdropping, the feature of the application modeller that should be used for scanning is the Application Navigator. This is because the Application Navigator scans the Application Model Tree for all the items it can locate, making it the best option in this scenario. Therefore, option A is the correct choice.

Option B, which suggests using DDE elements, is incorrect because DDE elements are used for interprocess communication in a Windows context, and are not related to scanning a Java-based application.

Option C, which suggests using HTC components, is also incorrect because this option is selected when the business object engages in a transaction with an application that makes use of HTC modules, and is not related to scanning a Java-based application.

Option D, which suggests using Diagnostics, is also incorrect because Diagnostics are used to diagnose and fix problems, and are not related to scanning an application. Therefore, option A (Application Navigator) is the best choice for this scenario.

Question 91:

As a Blue Prism developer, you are using the application modeller wizard to search for elements in a target Java application. Which option should you select to search the whole Application Model Tree for these elements?

A) Descendtree

B) Ignorenotshowing

C) Number of One's Ancestors, Subtract One

D) Contrary to Expectation

Explanation:

Answer - A

To search the whole Application Model Tree for elements in a target Java application using the application modeller wizard, you should select the Descendtree option. This option triggers Blue Prism to look through the full Program Model Tree for components in the target Java application. When this switch is off, Blue Prism only gets a list of visible Java items for each visible window in the target program. Therefore, option A is the correct choice.

Option B, which suggests using Ignorenotshowing, is incorrect because this option instructs Blue Prism to disregard child nodes in the Application Model Tree that are reported to be hidden.

Option C, which suggests using "Number of One's Ancestors, Subtract One," is also incorrect because this is not a valid option in the application modeller wizard.

Option D, which suggests a "Contrary to Expectation" option, is also incorrect because there is no such option in the application modeller wizard. Therefore, option A (Descendtree) is the best choice for this scenario.

Question 92:

As a Blue Prism developer, you need to work with PDF files and want to know which software is best suited for this purpose. Which of the following options should you choose?

A) Google Chrome

B) Internet Explorer

C) Acrobat PDF Reader

D) Word Processing Program

Explanation:

Answer - C

When working with PDF files, the best software option is Acrobat PDF Reader. This is because Adobe Acrobat's PDF reader is the recommended method of interacting with PDF files. Therefore, option C is the correct choice.

Option A, which suggests using Google Chrome, is incorrect because Google Chrome is used to connect with browser applications and is not the best software for working with PDF files.

Option B, which suggests using Internet Explorer, is also incorrect because using the internet to connect with browser-based software is not the best option for working with PDF files.

Option D, which suggests using a word processing program, is also incorrect because Microsoft Word is required to view and edit Word documents, not PDF files. Therefore, option C (Acrobat PDF Reader) is the best choice for this scenario.

Question 93:

As a Blue Prism developer, you need to regexptually extract the numbers from the text "I.D. NUMBER: 00012345678". Which order of operations should you use?

A) Your [s*([0-9])][(ID NUMBER:)].

B) The correct ID number format is B. [a-z]s([a-z]).

C) [(ID NUMBER:)]s[0-9]

D) None of the aforementioned

Explanation:

Answer - A

To regexptually extract the numbers from the text "I.D. NUMBER: 00012345678," you should use option A: Your [s*([0-9]*)][(ID NUMBER:)]. This regular expression pattern will match any sequence of digits after the text "ID NUMBER:," allowing you to extract the numbers from the text. Therefore, option A is the correct choice.

Option B, which suggests that the correct ID number format is [a-z]s*([a-z]*), is incorrect because this regular expression pattern will match only lowercase letters and spaces, and is not suitable for extracting numbers from the text.

Option C, which suggests using [(ID NUMBER:)]s[0-9]*, is also incorrect because this pattern will match any sequence of characters after "ID NUMBER:", including letters and special characters, and is not suitable for extracting only the numbers from the text.

Option D, which suggests that none of the above options are correct, is also incorrect because option A is the correct order of operations for regexptually extracting the numbers from the text.

Question 94:

As a Blue Prism developer, you need to handle confidential data and want to know which feature of Blue Prism is most appropriate for this purpose. Which of the following options should you choose?

A) Job Waiting List

B) Encryption

C) Credential Manager

D) Database

Explanation:

Answer - C

The most appropriate feature of Blue Prism for handling confidential data is the Credential Manager. This feature allows you to securely store and manage credentials, such as usernames and passwords, for accessing systems and applications. Therefore, option C is the correct choice.

Option A, which suggests using the Job Waiting List, is incorrect because work queues are used to automate work case items, not to handle confidential data.

Option B, which suggests using encryption, is also incorrect because encryption is not a module of Blue Prism and is not used to handle confidential data in this context.

Option D, which suggests using a database, is also incorrect because databases are not typically used to hold sensitive data in this context. Therefore, option C (Credential Manager) is the best choice for this scenario.

Question 95:

As a Blue Prism developer, you need to create a custom calendar and want to know which module of Blue Prism is suitable for this purpose. Which of the following options should you choose?

A) The Command Center

B) System Manager

C) Process Studio

D) Object Studio

Explanation:

Answer - B

To create a custom calendar in Blue Prism, you should use the System Manager module. This module allows you to create and manage custom calendars for scheduling tasks and processes. Therefore, option B is the correct choice.

Option A, which suggests using the Command Center, is incorrect because the Control Room is used to monitor the daily execution, queue status, and schedules, not to create custom calendars.

Option C, which suggests using Process Studio, is also incorrect because this module is used to create business logic and rules, not to create custom calendars.

Option D, which suggests using Object Studio, is also incorrect because this module is used to spy the target application's parts and to construct actions to interface with the application, not to create custom calendars. Therefore, option B (System Manager) is the best choice for this scenario.

Question 96:

As a Blue Prism developer, you want to know which espionage mode is often employed in surface automation. Which of the following options should you choose?

A) Active Accessibility (AA) mode

B) Win32 Mode

C) HTML Compatibility Mode

D) Region

Explanation:

Answer - D

In surface automation, the mode often employed for espionage is Region mode. This mode is used to capture images and automate thin client applications, making it an effective tool for surface automation. Therefore, option D is the correct choice.

Option A, which suggests using Active Accessibility (AA) mode, is incorrect because this mode is intended to be used with applications that do not expose their elements using Microsoft Active Accessibility.

Option B, which suggests using Win32 Mode, is also incorrect because this mode is typically used to spy on Windows applications running in Win32 mode.

Option C, which suggests using HTML Compatibility Mode, is also incorrect because this mode is used for web application spies that utilize HTML mode, not for surface automation. Therefore, option D (Region) is the best choice for this scenario.

Question 97:

As a Blue Prism developer, you need to install the Tesseract language files on the Blue Prism resource PC. Which of the following options should you choose?

A) C:\Program Files\Blue Prism Limited\Blue Prism Automate\Tesseract\tessdata

B) C:\Program Files\Blue Prism Limited\Blue Prism Automate\Tesseract\tessdata\languages

C) C:\Program Files\Blue Prism Limited\Blue Prism Automate\Tesseract

D) C:\Program Files\Blue Prism Limited\Blue Prism Automate\Tesseract\Languages

Explanation:

Answer - A

The correct answer is A. This is because the Tesseracttessdata folder located within the Blue Prism installation directory is where additional language support files should be placed after downloading them.

Option B is not correct because it points to a subfolder within the Tesseracttessdata directory, not the main directory itself.

Option C is not correct because it points to the Tesseract directory, not the Tesseracttessdata directory where the language files should be placed.

Option D is not correct because it is identical to option B, which is also incorrect.

Therefore, the correct option for installing the Tesseract language files on the Blue Prism resource PC is A.

Question 98:

A Blue Prism developer is tasked with automating data extraction from an insurance company's web application. The application provides policy information in both text and date formats. The developer wants to know which data type to use when reading character data from the application.

Which of the following is true regarding surface automation and data types for character data?

A) The Text data type is recommended for use even for numeric values like dates.

B) The Number data type is preferable for reading character data from an application, even for values like dates.

C) The Image data type is recommended for usage when reading character data from an application, including character data in date format.

D) None of the aforementioned options are correct.

Explanation:

Answer - A

The correct answer is A. Blue Prism recommends using the Text data type when reading character data from an application, even for numeric values like dates. This prevents casting errors and allows for easier troubleshooting after the fact. Option B is incorrect because the Number data type should only be used for numerical data, not character data. Option C is incorrect because the Image data type is not recommended for character data, including character data in date format. Option D is incorrect because there is only one correct option, which is A.

Question 99:

A Blue Prism developer is building a process that needs to call an external web service to retrieve data. The developer wants to know during which stage the web service methods should be called.

During which of the following stages should the methods of external web services be called in a Blue Prism process?

A) Action

B) Page

C) Subprocess

D) Calculation

Explanation:

Answer - A

The correct answer is A. Calls to external web service methods should be made during the Action stage of a Blue Prism process. This is the stage where the logic of the process is executed, including calling external services to retrieve or process data. Option B is incorrect because the Page stage is only used to access pages within the same process or object. Option C is incorrect because the Subprocess stage is used to initiate calls to other subprocesses. Option D is incorrect because the Calculation stage is where mathematical or logical computations take place within a process.

Question 100:

A company has built a process-based web service to handle customer data requests from external consumers. The company wants to know how the process-based web service can be initialized by its consumers.

What are the possible initialization methods for a process-based web application by its users?

A) 0

B) 1

C) 2

D) 3

Explanation:

Answer - A

The correct answer is A. Process-based web services only need to be executed once per instance, and there is only one point of entry.

Therefore, no initialization procedures are required, and the process-based web service can be initialized with zero ways by its consumers. Option B, C, and D are incorrect because there are no setup or teardown procedures required for process-based web services, and there is only one point of entry.

Question 101:

A Blue Prism developer has set up Process A to run in Exclusive mode on Machine1. Five web service requests are received in rapid succession, all of which are destined for the currently active Process B. What will be the outcome of these requests?

A) Process A will be halted while Process B is given access to the machine.

B) Five separate sessions will be started up on Machine1.

C) Six new sessions will be created on Machine1.

D) The five web service calls will be refused with this session.

Explanation:

Answer - D

The correct answer is D. Since Process A is running in Exclusive mode on Machine1, the active session is required for the execution of Process A. Therefore, new sessions cannot be created on Machine1 to handle the web service requests for Process B. As a result, the five web service calls will be refused with this session. Option A is incorrect because Process A will not be halted, and Process B cannot be given access to the machine. Option B and C are incorrect because new sessions cannot be created on Machine1.

Question 102:

A Blue Prism developer is working on a complex task queue management system that involves tags with asterisks. The developer wants to know which configuration is correct and how to use the Get Next Item Tag Filter feature to retrieve items with actual asterisks in their tags.

Which of the following configurations is correct, and how can the Get Next Item Tag Filter feature be used to retrieve items with actual asterisks in their tags?

A) "*"

B) "/"

C) "**"

D) "+"

Explanation:

Answer - C

The correct answer is C. The escape character is not supported by Blue Prism, so option A cannot be used. Option B is incorrect because the / character is not allowed in Blue Prism. Option C is correct because to search for literal asterisks, they can be escaped by inserting them in the search twice. For example, if the tag is "itemtag", the filter would be "**". Option D is incorrect because "+" would return cases labeled as "+*," not cases with actual asterisks in their tags.

Also by Exam OG

Microsoft Azure Fundamentals Exam AZ-900 Certification Concept Based Practice Question Latest Edition 2023

Microsoft Azure Fundamentals Exam AZ-900 Certification Case Based Practice Questions Latest Edition 2023

Concept Based Practice Questions for Tableau Desktop Specialist Certification Latest Edition 2023

Concept Based Practice Questions for Salesforce Administrator Certification Latest Edition 2023

Salesforce Administrator Certification Cased Based Practice Questions Latest Edition 2023

Concept Based Practice Questions for AWS Solutions Architect Certification Latest Edition 2023

AWS Solutions Architect Certification Cased Based Practice Questions Latest Edition 2023

Concept Based Practice Questions for UiPath RPA Associate Certification Latest Edition 2023

UiPath Certified RPA Associate Case Based Practice Questions Latest Edition 2023

Concept Based Practice Question for Blue Prism in Robotic Process Automation (RPA)

Blue Prism Developer Certification Case Based Practice Question - Latest 2023

Blue Prism Professional Developer Certification Case Based Practice Questions - Latest Edition 2023

Tableau Desktop Specialist Certification Case Base Practice Questions - Latest Edition 2023

www.ingramcontent.com/pod-product-compliance
Ingram Content Group UK Ltd.
Pitfield, Milton Keynes, MK11 3LW, UK
UKHW021534020325
4821UKWH00025B/107

9 798215 017272